Terezín
Theresienstadt

Litoměřice
Leitmeritz

To the Dead

A grave among graves, who can tell it apart,
time has long swept away the dead faces.
Testimonies, so evil and terrible to the heart,
we took with us to these dark rotting places.

Only the night and the howl of the wind
will sit on the graves' corners,
only a patch of grass, a bitter weed
before May bears some flowers...

JAROSLAV SEIFERT

Places of Suffering and Braveness

The facilities of Nazi repression in Terezín and Litoměřice

The foundation of the town of Terezín dates back to the late 18th century, when Emperor Josef II, drawing on his experience from several Prussian-Austrian wars, decided to build a fortress at the confluence of the Labe and Ohře Rivers. Its mission was to prevent any future penetration of enemy forces into the Bohemian interior along the Dresden-Lovosice-Prague route, as well as guard the Labe waterway. The stronghold, built over the period of ten years, consisted of the Main and the Small Fortress, alongside a fortified area between the New and Old Ohře Rivers. The fortification consisted of a number of elements – massive bastions, ravelins, lunettes, bulwarks, flood-moats and an extensive network of underground passages. The basins, occupying two-thirds of the surrounding belt of the fortress, could also be flooded. The stronghold, however, was never used in battle and its fortifications, practically impregnable at the time of construction, gradually grew obsolete. Finally, the fortress was vacated and Terezín turned into a garrison town. It took little time in the 19th century for the penitentiary within the Small Fortress to gain a notorious reputation. It functioned well into the first half of the 20th century: during WWI, it held a number of the Habsburg Monarchy's enemies including the Sarajevo assassins, and served as a military prison and penitentiary for a full twenty years after Czechoslovak independence in 1918.

Terezín registered with the world's public during and after WWII as one of the symbols of persecution of the political enemies of Hitler's Germany, as well as the implementation of the monstrous genocide programme against European Jews.

Terezín's Small Fortress became a police prison of the Prague Gestapo in June 1940 – mostly political prisoners were detained there. Thousands of members of various resistance movement groups from the occupied Czech lands as well as other countries passed through its gates.

The town itself – the former Main Fortress – was turned into a ghetto, collection and transit camp for Jews in November 1941. At first Jews from the then Protectorate of Bohemia and Moravia were deported here, later also from the Reich (Germany, Austria) and other countries.

A branch of the Flossenbürg concentration camp was opened in nearby Litoměřice in the spring of 1944. It was the charge of its prisoners to build underground factories and, subsequently, to serve as slave labour in the production.

Over 200,000 people from 30 countries were imprisoned in these three facilities of repression between 1940 and 1945. Every fifth prisoner died in one of them, and as many as 90,000 died after being deported to other places of suffering. Many lives ended in extermination and concentration camps, prisons and penitentiaries, and mass execution sites.

The end of the war, however, was not to be an end to the suffering and mass death in Terezín and Litoměřice. From late April to early May 1945, during the Nazi retreat which brought thousands of evacuated prisoners from the concentration camps, epidemics of spotted fever and other diseases started. As a result, many liberated prisoners, doctors and medical personnel including former prisoners, as well as members of Czech Action for Help (volunteers from Prague and other places), and members of the Red Army, died weeks after the war ended. Thanks to the immeasurable effort and sacrifices of physicians and medical personnel, the spotted fever epidemic was halted and 25,000 were saved from death. Afterwards, former prisoners were allowed to repatriate from the end of May to mid August 1945.

On the initiative of the newly created Czechoslovak government, in 1947 the National Suffering Memorial was opened on the site of the suffering of tens of thousands; it was later on renamed the Terezín Memorial.

TEREZÍN SMALL FORTRESS

The Small Fortress originated as a stronghold, above all designed to guard the Labe waterway and the weir locks of the fortification flooding system. Soon after completion, it also began to function as the so-called Festungs-Stockhaus – a military penitentiary, and shortly afterwards political prisoners who opposed the Habsburg Monarchy were also held here.

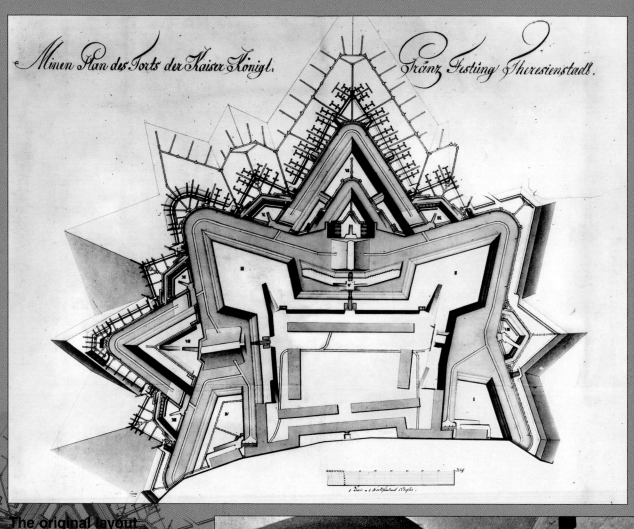

The original layout of the Small Fortress

The old prison cells of the Small Fortress, built after 1830

The Small Fortress functioned as the Habsburg Monarchy jail also during WWI. Its prisoners included the plotters of the Sarajevo Assassination, which was the impetus for the First World War. Most of them perished in this prison.
In 1915–1918, barrack camps were built near Terezín for Russian, Serbian, Italian and Romanian prisoners of war.

The cell in which Gavrilo Princip, the main protagonist of the Sarajevo Assassination, was imprisoned and died 1918

Russian WWI captives in Terezín

Approximately 2,500 prisoners walked the yards of the Small Fortress during WWI, including about 560 participants of 7th Riflemen Regiment Mutiny in Rumburk. In 1914–1915, over a thousand so-called Russophils, i. e. the Ruthenian inhabitants of Galicia, Bukovina and Ruthenia were preventively held captive here for suspicion of support to enemy Russia.

A group of Ruthenians interned in the Small Fortress

A group of the Rumburk Mutiny participants, imprisoned in the Small Fortress

One of the corridors of the old Terezín fortification

TEREZÍN SMALL FORTRESS

The years of the Nazi occupation of the Czech lands were the most tragic chapter of the Small Fortress. A police prison of Prague's Gestapo was established here as early as June 1940. Roughly 32,000 prisoners went through its ever more crowded cells. Famine, epidemics, inhuman treatment, and executions ended 2,600 lives, including those of 500 women. Another 5,500 prisoners died after deportations to Nazi concentration camps, penitentiaries and prisons.

Violence and death ruled within the gates of the Small Fortress

The prisoners' journey from the train station in Bohušovice nad Ohří to the Small Fortress (the only authentic photograph of arriving prisoners from the period of occupation)

The Small Fortress entrance gate with a moat

A view of the Administration Courtyard with offices. This was where the prisoners first faced the warders' despotic manners during the reception procedure

The prisoner reception and registration office (current look after reconstruction)

The First Courtyard, where the roll calls took place. The office in the front left corner belonged to warder Rojko, nicknamed "The Executioner of Terezín"

Solitary cells in the First Courtyard. Prisoners with serious penalties were put in these cold cells, often naked. Their suffering was made worse by the withholding of provisions, torture, and often total darkness

Prisoner roll call in the First Courtyard

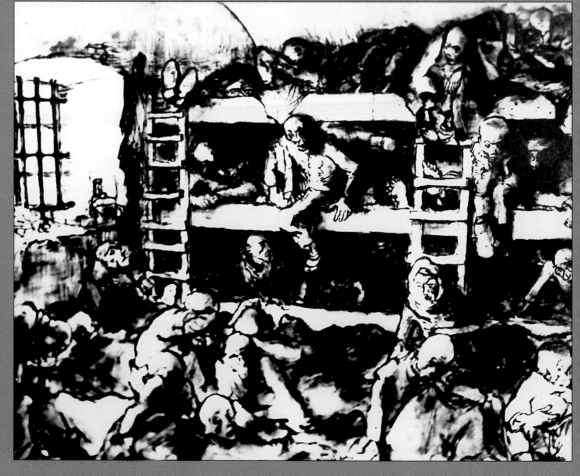

The little yard by the solitary cells, where a number of prisoners were brutally tortured to death

Jewish prisoners in the Small Fortress, painted by Leo Haas. They were sent here for being members of the resistance movement and for violations of Anti-Jewish regulations or Ghetto camp rules. They were treated with extraordinary cruelty

The Women's Courtyard in the Small Fortress. Solitary cells on the right

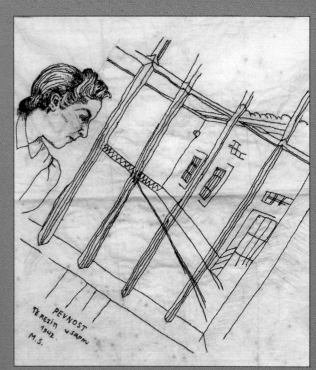

An embroidery by an unknown woman prisoner, bearing the initials M. S., dated August 1942

Cell no. 28 was used as working space, where women painted wooden buttons, mended sacks, and bound queues used for making slippers

A view of wire blocks and the watchtower of the Fourth Courtyard

The prisoners' personal records contained, besides the reason for arrest, also the date of arrival to and departure from Terezín, including remarks on their transport to concentration camps

Lfd. Nr.: *21705*

41

Haft Nr.: **1658**

G. K. K.:

Karteikarte.

Zuname: **Štol**

Vorname: **Josef**

Beruf: **Schlosser**

Geburtstag: **16.2.00**

Geburtsort: **Kolin**

Staatsangehöriger: **Prot.**

Wohnung: **Kolin VII- 398**

Familienstand: **verh.**

Religion: **r.k.**

Einlieferungsstelle: **Kolin**

wegen : **deutschfeindl. Propaganda**

Tag der Einlieferung: *2. XI. 1944* Uhr: *17*

Beendigung der Haft: *9. XII. 1944* Uhr: *18*

Grund der Haftbeendigung: *Transport el. entlassungsbefehl d. Kds Prag v. 6.12.44 IV6b S 2470 - KL Flossenburg*

Quittung des Häftlings: *Josf Stol*

Hafttage: *41*

The Fourth Courtyard, nicknamed by the prisoners "Small Fortress's Grave". It was built in 1943–1944 and over 3,000 prisoners were narrowly surviving and dying here towards the end of the war

The execution corner of the Fourth Courtyard. After an attempt at flight from cell no. 38 on March 3, 1945, four prisoners were shot here

In the so-called kites or secretly sent out scrolls, the prisoners were trying to give testimonies of the real conditions in the prison. If this connection to the outside world was revealed, brutal punishment followed

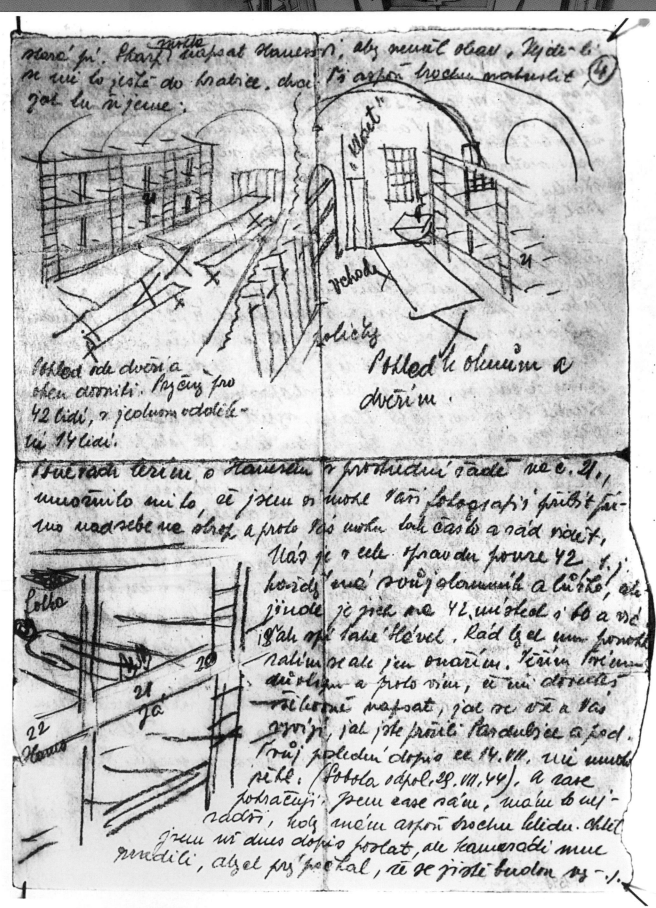

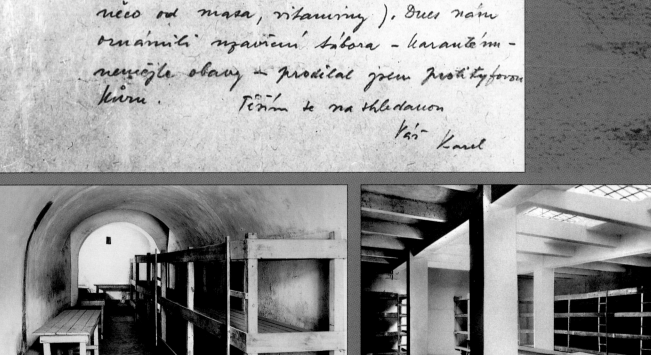

Cell no. 38 was situated directly inside the fortification mound. In the last months of the war, 50 to 60 prisoners were crowded into it

Cell no. 44 in the Fourth Courtyard, called "The Death Cell". Between 400 and 600 prisoners were packed in horrible conditions in this as well as each of the other collective cells

The prisoners' workforce was systematically used for hard labour. They were only working inside the prison at first, but later on more and more so-called external gangs were employed in agriculture, industry and road works.

The swimming pool for the warders and their children, built by the prisoners. Its construction saw continuous torture, maltreatment and beating of the prisoners to death. Behind the pool, the so-called Manor House can be seen with the warders' and director's flats

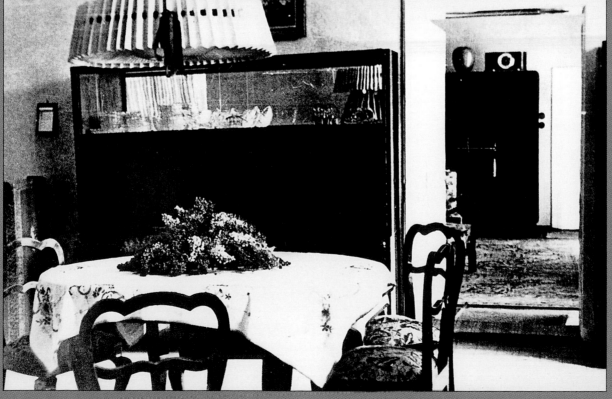

Interior of the flat of Heinrich Jöckel, the prison commander and the absolute ruler of the Small Fortress. Its luxurious rooms are in sharp contrast to the humiliating conditions of the cells

The departure of
a labour gang

Terezín prisoners working
at the railway station
in Ústí nad Labem

Desperate hygiene and health conditions in the Small Fortress deteriorated day by day due to cell overcrowding, poor provisions and a lack of water, and they became untenable by the end of 1944.

A drawing by Josef Kylies: Prisoners looking for fleas. In spite of all prisoners' efforts it was impossible to get rid of insects in the Small Fortress, namely fleas spreading spotted fever

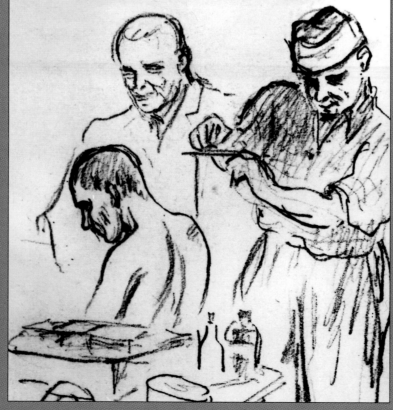

A drawing by Josef Kylies: MUDr. Poňka operating using a razor blade in cell 41. Especially in the Fourth Courtyard, prisoner-physicians were left with next to no medical supplies or equipment in 1944–1945. Nevertheless, they kept trying to help their fellow prisoners, even in these harsh conditions

The executions held in the Small Fortress rank among crimes never to be forgotten. Under the so-called sonderbehandlung (special treatment), over 250 people were put to death here without trial from 1943 on.

The execution area of the Small Fortress. As late as May 2, 1945, execution squads ended the lives of 51 prisoners (including the confident Jaroslav Fiala, an inconvenient witness)

The bodies of 601 prisoners were exhumed from mass graves in the Small Fortress in late summer of 1945

The brutal crime in the Small Fortress was mainly committed by the SS-warders, headed by their commander, a mass murderer and criminal of war, Heinrich Jöckel. He and most warders were deservedly punished after the war ended, but many escaped justice.

Heinrich Jöckel in the prison's heyday

Heinrich Jöckel immediately before execution

122

Jöckel with the
warders in the
Small Fortress, 1941

TEREZÍN GHETTO

A key part of the Nazi plans for the New Order of Europe was extermination of all Jews within the reach of Hitler's Germany. A Ghetto, a collection and transit camp for the Jewish population was established in Terezín on November 24, 1941. The Terezín Ghetto became an important cog in the monstrous machine of the "Final Solution of the Jewish Question", as the euphemistic Nazi title for the Jewish genocide ran. All civilians had to leave Terezín by mid 1942. Whereas the imprisoned Jews had been held in barrack buildings before this date, the entire town now became a large prison. Jews from the then Protectorate of Bohemia and Moravia were deported here first, but later also from the Reich (Germany, Austria), the Netherlands, Denmark, Slovakia and Hungary. In addition, prisoners from many countries arrived here in the very end of the war with the so-called evacuation transports and death marches from concentration camps being evacuated as the war front proceeded. In total, more than 155,000 men, women and children went through the gates of the Ghetto. About 35,000 of them found death in Terezín; another 83,000 died after deportations from Terezín in extermination camps, concentration camps and death marches towards the war's end.

Transports of Jewish prisoners on the way from the railway station in Bohušovice nad Ohří to Terezín

The transports were being escorted by special Czech gendarmerie troops

Bedřich
Fritta:
Transport
of prisoners

Charlotta
Burešová:
Transport
of prisoners

The SS Camp Command had absolute power over the lives of the prisoners. Its members terrorised the imprisoned both psychologically and physically. A prisoner's everyday life was bound by an entire system of orders and prohibitions.

Bunkers under the SS Camp Command, where the prisoners were interrogated and tortured

Leo Haas: Members of the SS Camp Command

Sixteen prisoners were hanged on this gallows for minor offences in January and February 1942

The Jewish self-administration, created in Terezín as well as other ghettos and concentration camps, was in charge of the internal functioning of the Ghetto and the obedience to the SS Camp Command – issued orders and prohibitions.

Jakob Edelstein – one of the three Elders of the Jews of the Terezín Ghetto. He was replaced with Paul Eppstein in January 1943, and shot in Auschwitz together with his wife and son in June 1944

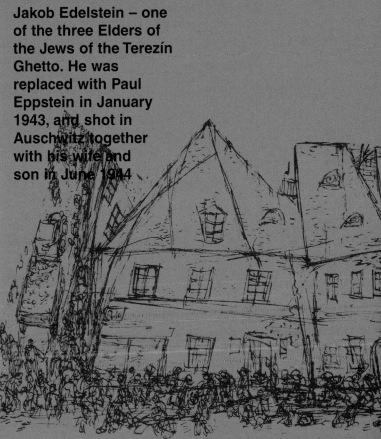

Paul Eppstein (standing) delivering a speech in the Council of Elders. He was shot in the Small Fortress in September 1944 and Benjamin Murmelstein (sitting on his left) replaced him until the war's end

It was the duty of the special Czech gendarmerie unit to guard the Ghetto boundaries and to escort prisoners outside these boundaries. Its members were on duty in Terezín for a period of three to six months.

Special Czech Protectorate gendarmerie unit during a roll call in the courtyard of the former officers' casino

Gendarmes guarding Terezín's mounds

TEREZÍN GHETTO

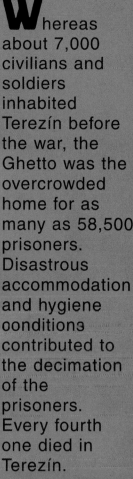

Whereas about 7,000 civilians and soldiers inhabited Terezín before the war, the Ghetto was the overcrowded home for as many as 58,500 prisoners. Disastrous accommodation and hygiene conditions contributed to the decimation of the prisoners. Every fourth one died in Terezín.

Bedřich Fritta: A ghetto street

A Hannover Barracks dormitory with three-storey bunks

There were a number of old and powerless prisoners
in the Terezín Ghetto, whose fate was especially hard.
A drawing by Bedřich Fritta captures a transport
of the elderly to the dormitories on a funeral cart

A drawing
by Bedřich
Fritta: The
"homes" of
the elderly
prisoners
in the attic

Otto Ungar:
The disabled
in the Ghetto

Moritz Müller:
Old women
taking rest

Atypical feature of the everyday life in the Ghetto was hunger: it took on the form of long-term under-nourishment. It was caused not only by the insufficient volume of food, but also by its monotony, and a lack of vitamins.

A prisoner's voucher for garbage vegetables. All usable vegetables were delivered to the SS kitchen, or exported from the Ghetto

Leo Haas: Waiting for food

Prisoners worked in many places inside the Ghetto, and external gangs were often sent to more or less distant surroundings.

Bedřich Fritta: Construction site labour

Leo Haas: A joiner's workshop

Otto Ungar: Railway siding construction

The transports were a reason for trauma to all prisoners. They did not only arrive in the Ghetto, but starting from January 1942, they were also taking prisoners away "to the East" – no one really knew where. In fact, they were mostly headed for places of extermination and slave labour in the occupied parts of Poland and Soviet Union. Auschwitz was almost invariably the destination after the end of October 1942.

3047 561/Cn   Hirsch Irma   1900   Langestr.5/200   A V

EINBERUFUNG

Sie wurden in den Transport eingereiht und haben sich zur Abfertigung pünktlich lt. Angabe des Gebäude-bezw. Hausältesten am Sammelplatz einzustellen.
Der Sammelplatz Ihrer Gruppe ist im rechten oberen Eck dieser Einberufung (an letzter Stelle des aufgeklebten Streifens) angegeben.

Nach Erhalt dieser Einberufung müssen Sie sofort Ihr Gepäck vorbereiten. Der Umfang des mitzunehmenden Gepäcks muss auf das allernotwendigste Mindestmass herabgesetzt werden. Keineswegs kann mehr als 1 Koffer oder 1 Weichgepäckstück mitgenommen werden. Grundsätzlich ist das Gepäck in die Schleuse persönlich mitzunehmen.

Schleussenantritt 17.12.43,10 h früh

Irma Hirsch's summons note for transport from Terezín to Auschwitz

Leo Haas: Waiting for transport

Charlotta Burešová:
Transported

A new railway siding from Bohušovice nad Ohří station to Terezín made it possible to receive and dispatch transports directly in the Ghetto. This picture was taken on the arrival of the first train on June 1, 1943

The Ghetto health care system started in extremely difficult conditions. At first, doctors and medical staff were able to carry out the most complicated operations only with primitive equipment, permanently lacking medication and bandages. The situation gradually improved only thanks to the fact that some of the inventory could be used that was confiscated from Jewish doctors' surgeries in fear of possible epidemics. However, the lack of medication and other material was permanent, and not even the self-denial of the doctors could prevent death from taking its high toll.

Norbert Troller:
Operation

Otto Ungar:
A Prayer for a Dead

Ghetto Theresienstadt
Der Ältestenrat.

Theresienstadt, am 8.2.1942.

Tagesbefehl Nr.46
vom 8. Feber 1942.

1.) Postverkehr

Laut Anordnung des Herrn SS Obersturmbandführer Eichmann dürfen
Briefe und Karten nur in Blockschrift geschrieben sein und nur
30 Worte enthalten.

Es wird zugleich noch einmal darauf aufmerksam gemacht,

a) dass Briefe an Ghettoinsassen nur im Wege der Jüdischen Kultusgemeinde Prag geschrieben werden können. Poststücke, wel-
che nicht durch die Jüdische Kultusgemeinde Prag gehen, son-
dern direkt auf der Post aufgegeben werden, werden im Ghetto
nicht zugestellt.

b) dass die einlangenden Poststücke nur in deutscher Sprache zu-
lässig sind,

c) Angaben über die Zahl der Ghettoinsassen zu unterbleiben haben,

d) Hinweise auf Paketsendungen vorderhand zu unterlassen sind.

2.) Bettenbau

Die Werkstätten der Wirtschaftsabteilung haben bis zum heutigen
Tage insgesamt 1421 Bettstellen fertiggestellt und in der Sudeten-
kaserne montiert.

3.) Todesfälle

Am 7. Feber 1942 war kein Todesfall zu verzeichnen.

Der Ältestenrat.
i.A.

The SS Camp Command took all effort to conceal from the outer world the truth about real life in the Terezín Ghetto and its purpose. All mail was strictly censored, and all attempts at communication with the outside world were punished drastically.

The prisoner out-of-the-ghetto postage principles were set in person by the head of the Jewish Department of Berlin's Gestapo Central, Adolf Eichmann

A post-card sent from the Terezín Ghetto

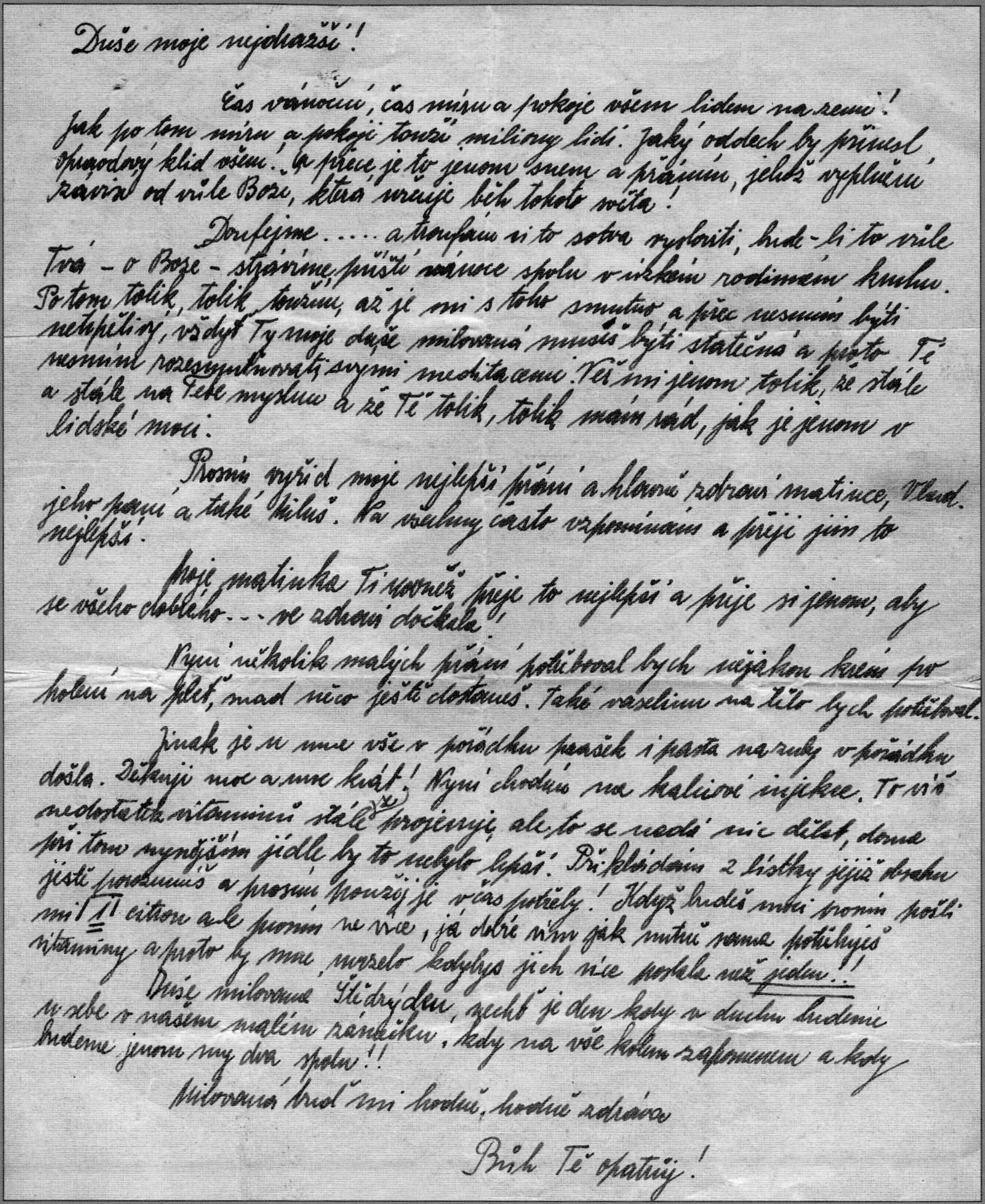

Duše moje nejdražší!

Čas vánoční, čas míru a pokoje všem lidem na zemi! Jak po tom míru a pokoji touží miliony lidí. Jaký oddech by přinesl opravdový klid všem. A přece je to jenom snem a přáním, jehož vyplnění závisí od vůle Boží, která určuje běh tohoto světa!

Doufejme ..... a troufám si to sotva vysloviti, bude-li to vůle Tvá – o Bože – strávíme, příští vánoce spolu v úzkém rodinném kruhu. Po tom tolik, tolik toužím, až je mi s toho smutno a přec nesmím býti netrpělivý, vždyť Ty moje duše milovaná musíš býti statečná a proto Tě nesmím rozesmutňovati svými meditacemi. Věř mi jenom tolik, že stále a stále na Tebe myslím a že Tě tolik, tolik mám rád, jak je jenom v lidské moci.

Prosím vyřiď moje nejlepší přání a hlavně zdraví matince, Vlad. jeho paní a také Miluš. Na všechny často vzpomínám a přeji jim to nejlepší.

Moje matinka Ti srdečně přeje to nejlepší a přeje si jenom, aby se všeho dobrého ... ve zdraví dočkala!

Nyní několik malých přání potřeboval bych nějakou krémi po holení na pleť, mad něco ještě dostaneš. Také vazelínu na tělo bych potřeboval.

Jinak je u mne vše v pořádku psaček i pasta na ruky v pořádku došla. Děkuji moc a moc krát! Nyní chodím na kalciové injekce. To s ní nedostatek vitaminů stále [x] projevují, ale to se nedá nic dělat, doma při tom vydatějším jídle by to nebylo lepší! Přikládám 2 lístky jejíž druhu ještě porozumíš a prosím použij je včas potřeby! Když budeš mít prosím pošli mi [II] citron ale prosím ne více, já dobře vím jak nutně sama potřebuješ vitaminy a proto by mne mrzelo kdybys jich více poslala než jeden!!

Duše milovaná Štědrý den, zechť je den kdy v duchu budeme u sebe v našem malém zámečku, kdy na vše kolem zapomenem a kdy budeme jenom my dva spolu!!

Milovaná tvůj mi hodně, hodně zdráva

Bůh Tě opatruj!

An uncensored letter smuggled illegally out of the Ghetto

Admission postage stamp for Terezín. All incoming mail to the Ghetto had to be stamped with one. The numbers of free people outside, to which the prisoners could send one (if they themselves got hold of one), unfortunately shrunk quickly

As part of the preparations for a visit by an international delegation, to serve the propaganda of Hitler's Germany and obscure the reality of the "Final Solution of the Jewish Question", Terezín went through a so-called Beautification Action in 1943–1944. The overall appearance of the buildings and prisoners' dormitories was improved, and facilities were built that were not normally accessible to the prisoners. Following the International Red Cross Committee delegation's visit, the scene for this megalomaniac theatre show was used for shooting a propaganda film to portray Terezín as an "autonomous Jewish settlement".

The children's home, established in the Ghetto prior to the International Red Cross Committee delegation's visit

The Music Pavilion in the square, built during the "Beautification Action"

The so far standard orders of the day were replaced with the new "Notices of the Jewish self-administration"

Adult prisoners did as much as they could to mitigate the hard fate of the Ghetto's children and youth. In the collective dormitories called homes (heims), tutors selected by the Jewish self-administration took as much care as possible – playing, painting, holding discussions and secretly teaching the older children.

The school building was converted into the 10–15 year old boys' homes

– 94 –

Vedem 15

časopis domova I. – Dne 26. března 1943.

Budeme míti odznak. – Smě.

Odznakem našeho domova bude kruh o vnitřním průměru 8 mm a vnějším XX mm. 3milimetrový pás z lesklého kovu ohraničuje tento kruh, který bude odznakem, symbolem našeho domova. Jsme kolektiv mladých chlapců, ztroskotavších na ostrově Terezíně, ale i když jsme trosečníky, jsme mladými odhodlanými muži, kteří v práci, v boji a ve hře, ruku v ruce tvoří nové hodnoty. Jsme kruhem, vypadne-li někdo z našeho středu, zradí-li nás, padne-li v boji, kruh se uzavře. Kruh, to je něco nekonečného, věčného. A přece matematika definovala přesně kruh. Jsme mladí, chceme žít, musíme žít, budeme žít. Naší úlohou je předat štafetu života příští generaci, naším cílem je, aby tato štafeta byla předána svobodnými muži a ženami, svobodným lidem. Tančíme na ostrově ztroskotanců kolem ohně, v jehož záři spatříme zítřek. Víru v budoucnost, tanec kamarádství, kamarádství v práci, v boji, ve hře. Slibujeme, že nezradíme kruh své jednoty, že síla každého jednotlivce, bude silou celku a síla celku silou jednotlivce. Slibujeme, že nezradíme svobody, která je nám více, než symbolem, za krajíc chleba shořčici a uherským sa-

The front page of one of the issues of Vedem, a magazine published by the boys in Home no. 1 in the former Terezín school

An ensemble of theatre puppets, made in the Terezín Ghetto

The poster advertising the children's opera Brundibár (Bumble Bee), which was played 55 times in total in the Ghetto

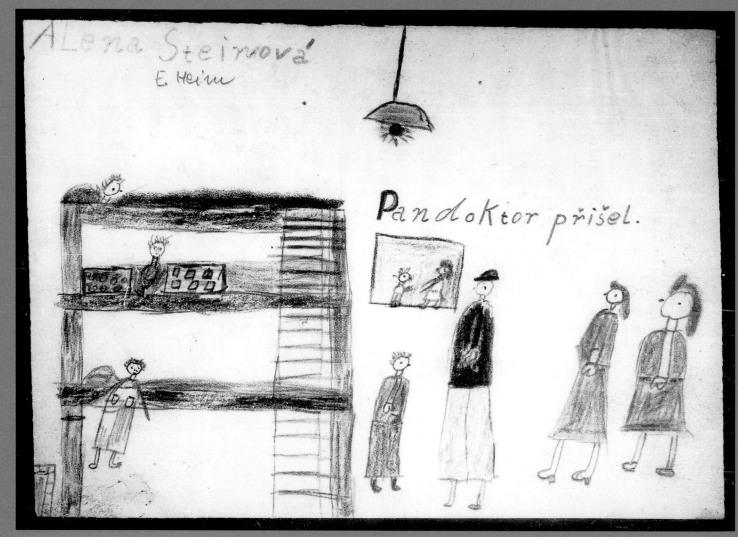

The only thing usually left behind by the many thousand children held prisoner in the Terezín Ghetto were their drawings – permanent proof of the Nazi atrocities

The ever-present hunger, epidemics of contagious diseases, terror by the SS guards and the psychic traumas related to them, work overload, and permanent overcrowding of the dormitories – all these factors kept the death rate among the prisoners high. It resulted soon in the building of a Terezín crematorium.

© Jewish Museum in Prague, inv. no. 175367, first edition 1984

Karel Fleischmann: In the Morgue

Burials in the mass graves of the Jewish Cemetery in summer 1942, when the death rate grew to catastrophic dimensions. A total of 9,000 people were buried here

The dead were cremated in the newly constructed crematorium from autumn 1942 on. Its furnaces swallowed a total of 30,000 victims of the Ghetto, the police prison in the Small Fortress, and the concentration camp in Litoměřice

The Jewish Cemetery immediately after Terezín's liberation

As the war front was receding towards the end of the war, concentration camps were evacuated and their prisoners put in the so-called evacuation transports. Their members travelled in open railway carriages, with nothing to eat or drink, brutally terrorised by the guards. Terezín became one of the destinations for these transports, as well as death marches, on April 20, 1945. Gradually, more than 15,000 new prisoners arrived here, bringing with them an epidemic of typhus.

The evacuees invariably arrived exhausted and disoriented, and many were seriously ill or dying. Many others did not survive transport

The arched vault of the unique Jewish room of prayer, furnished by the Ghetto's prisoners in a former warehouse

The remains of the railway siding that brought and dispatched the transport trains

The interior of the crematorium within the Jewish Cemetery

The Ceremonial Rooms where the last parting ceremonies were held, and the entrance to the Central Ghetto Morgue

The present-day look of the former Ghetto Columbarium

One part of the restored Central Ghetto Morgue with original coffins

The piously restored spaces of the Central Ghetto Morgue

LITOMĚŘICE CONCENTRATION

A concentration camp was founded in Litoměřice in 1944 – a branch of the main camp in Flossenbürg. Its prisoners built underground factories with the code names Richard I and Richard II. Nearly 18,000 prisoners – most of whom were Polish, Yugoslavian and Soviet – went through the camp. The number of prisoners coming from the Czech lands was relatively small. On the contrary, Jews from many European countries constituted a substantial share. The horrific conditions in which the prisoners had to live are best documented by the fact that approximately 4,500 people died here.

Litoměřice concentration camp watchtower (photographed in 1945)

The large number of dead made it necessary to build a crematorium

Exhumation of the largest mass grave near Litoměřice concentration camp. April 1946

The main access passage to the underground factory

Cargo transfer yard and railway station near the construction site

The interior of Litoměřice concentration camp crematorium

The furnaces of Litoměřice concentration camp crematorium

A view of the area of the former Litoměřice concentration camp

The main entrance to the former underground factory

Engine parts production was started in these underground spaces in November 1944. The machinery and all other equipment of the factory was taken away by the Red Army in 1945 as war bounty

Ventilation shaft. The entire underground was equipped by an ingenious forced ventilation system

Objects found underground tell tales of the prisoners' lives and work

The camp was dissolved some time before the liberation of Litoměřice. Its destruction was preceded by a dramatic evacuation of most of the prisoners, commenced in late April 1945 and only ended on 8 May by the liberation of a prisoner train near České Budějovice.

The prisoners kept fleeing from the evacuation train all along its route, and the Czech locals provided them with hiding and aid. In Roztoky u Prahy alone, over 300 prisoners fled, and the local inhabitants secured healthcare for them

Dead prisoners in train carriages, Roztoky u Prahy

Combating the Typhus Epidemic

The very end of the war saw the Gestapo police prison and Ghetto in Terezín as well as the Litoměřice concentration camp swept by an epidemic of typhus. It was brought here by the evacuation transports and death marches, which started en masse on April 20, 1945. The epidemic broke out first in the Litoměřice camp, from where it was transferred to the Small Fortress. It did not take long before it spread to the Ghetto too. The SS powers were already rapidly tumbling down in all three places at that time. Starting on 4 May, volunteers from among Czech doctors and medical staff, the members of Czech Action for Help, could work in the Small Fortress. The last SS men left Terezín one day later. Even after liberation, the medical staff was fighting with the epidemic in the Small Fortress, the former Ghetto, and the Litoměřice concentration camp.

One of the cells of the Fourth Courtyard, most severely plagued with spotted fever

Bathing and flea eradication of sick prisoners in the Small Fortress, assisted by Czech doctors and medical staff who came to the Small Fortress on May 4, 1945, as volunteers with Czech Action for Help

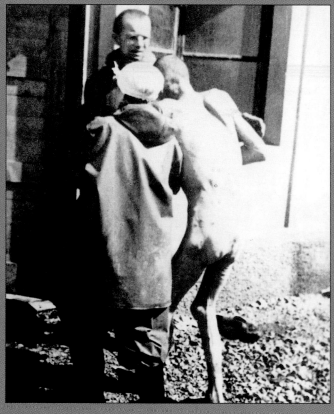

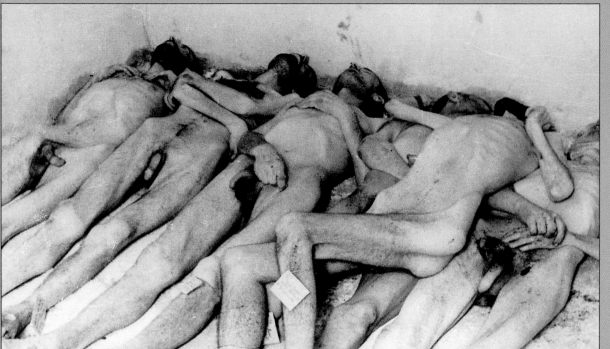

The epidemic claimed hundreds of victims in the Small Fortress

Evacuation transports and victims of death marches arrived at the Small Fortress

An emergency hospital set up in the Small Fortress

Wooden benches instead of hospital beds, a bowl and a few rags, were at first the primitive equipment of the provisional sick rooms. Sick prisoners from here were slowly moved to the emergency hospital in the former ghetto, starting on May 7, 1945

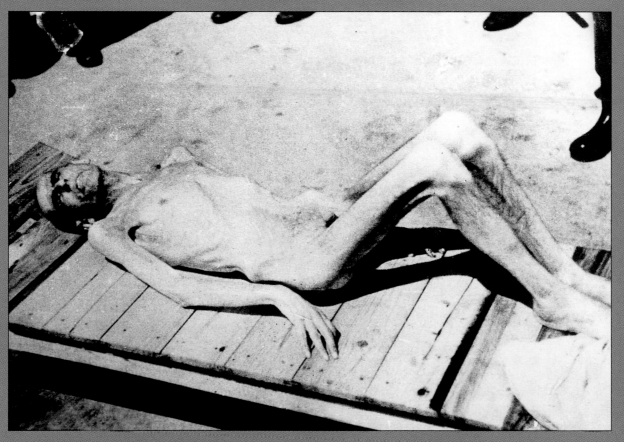

He survived prison in the Small Fortress

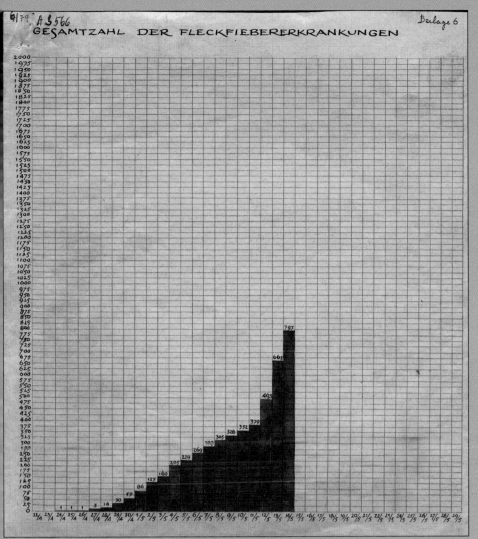

GESAMTZAHL DER FLECKFIEBERERKRANKUNGEN

Beilage 6

This graph shows
a sharp increase in the
number of spotted fever
cases in the Terezín
Ghetto in late
April and early
May 1945

A call of the Council of
Elders to the Ghetto's
women to make ready the
Sudeten Barracks in
Terezín town for reception
of spotted fever patients
from the Small Fortress

Správe budov .
/Gebäudeleitung ./

4.května 1945 .

Všem ženám československé příslušnosti !

Do našeho sídliště právě přibyli důstojníci zdravotnické
služby a sestry Českého Červeného Kříže aby převzali ošetření
nemocných českých příslušníků, kteří v nejbližších hodinách
budou v tak zvaných Sudetských kasárnách umístěni.

Správa budov převzala úkol tuto budovu v uvedené krátké
době vyčistititi a učiniti ji způsobilou k umístění nemocných.
Správa budov apeluje na ženy československé příslušnosti aby
ihned nastoupily k práci a provedli ji rychle a řádně. Je věcí
cti naších českých žen aby byly pohotovými a uvedený úkol do
důsledku splnily. Žádná z naších žen nesmí chyběti a každá nastoupí
dnes po 18. hodině večer k uvedené práci v Sudetských kasárnách.

Správa budov .

After the Liberation

The first Soviet tanks, headed for Prague, ran through Terezín on May 8, 1945. Two days later, the Red Army took over the town officially, which was still ravaged by the typhus epidemic. Former Ghetto prisoners were being treated in the town's provisional hospitals alongside evacuation transports. Also the sick from the Small Fortress were gradually being transferred here. The former Ghetto doctors were fighting the epidemic together with Czech Action for Help volunteers and Red Army medical personnel. The latter founded five field hospitals in Terezín and organised the supply of provisions and medicines. Nonetheless, the epidemic still claimed hundreds of lives among the liberated prisoners, and dozens of physicians and medical workers also died.

Terezín welcoming the Red Army

Major M. A. Kuzmin was appointed the military commander of Terezín

Aid was
pouring to
Terezín from
all sides

The entire city
turned into a vast
infections
hospital

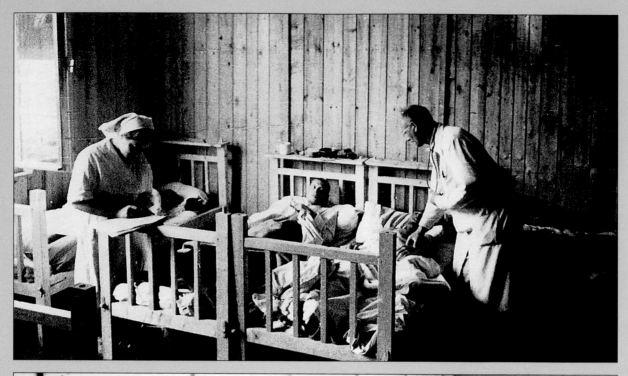

A doctor and nurse visiting the sick

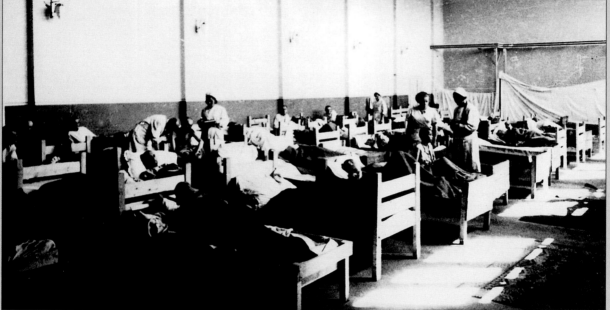

The interior of one of the provisional hospitals set up during the typhus epidemic

The buildings of the former Litoměřice concentration camp had to be burnt down after the liberation, due to their typhus contamination and insect infestation

Typical state of the liberated prisoners of the Litoměřice concentration camp

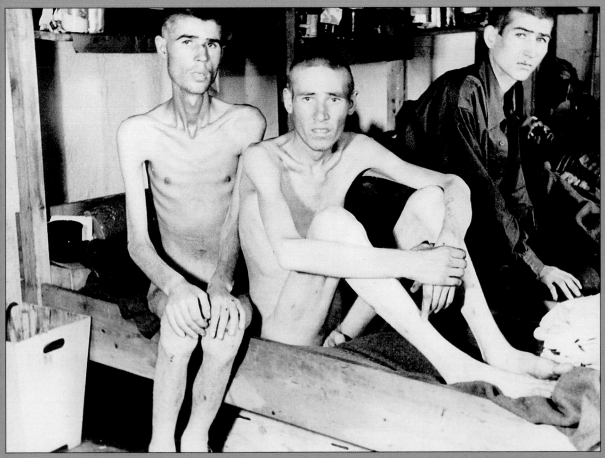

A provisional hospital in the former SS barracks in the Litoměřice concentration camp

We Do Not Forget

It is the primary purpose of the Terezín Memorial to stand in memory of the victims of the Nazi occupation and the suffering of the prisoners of the facilities of repression in Terezín and Litoměřice. It is commissioned to take care of the memorial places connected to this tragic chapter of our modern history, and to conduct museum, research, documentation and collection work. It is also active in education and public awareness. More than 250,000 domestic and international visitors are welcomed in the Terezín Memorial every year.

A National Funeral for the 601 victims exhumed from the mass graves of the Small Fortress took place on September 16, 1945. It was the basis for the founding of the Terezín National Cemetery. Since 1946, annual commemoration ceremonies have been held in this place every third Sunday of May

The bodily remains of the prisoners exhumed at Terezín, Litoměřice and Lovosice were transported to the Terezín National Cemetery until 1958. The bodily remains of the victims of the last Terezín execution were brought here from the Litoměřice crematorium in autumn 1945 (shown)

Dozens of volunteers participated in the gradual construction of the National Cemetery. They congregated under the National Cemetery Maintenance Association

Thirteen obelisks of the Avenue of the Nations, bearing the names of the countries whose citizens suffered and died in Terezín. They neighbour on the Jewish Cemetery crematorium

The entrance to the First Courtyard of the Gestapo police prison

A place of commemoration by the Ohře River. The ashes of 22,000 victims, cremated in Terezín, were ordered by the SS Camp Command to be thrown into the river

Annual commemoration ceremonies for the tortured Jewish prisoners are held at the Jewish Cemetery

Soviet Soldiers Memorial in Terezín, containing the graves of 49 Red Army soldiers

ARBEITSLAGER LEITMERITZ Kommando B.5.

Reichsdeutsche	polit.	▼	RD.Jud.	▲	
„	B.V.	▼	„	▼	
„	S.V.	▲	„	▲	
„	A.S.	▼		▼	
Polen	polit.	▼	P. Jud.	▲	
„	B.V.	▼	„	▼	
„	S.V.	▲	„	▼	
„	A.S.	▼	„	▼	
Russen	polit.	▼	R. Jud.	▲	
„	B.V.		„	▼	
„	S.V.	▲	„	▲	
„	A.S.	▼	„	▼	
Jugoslaven	polit.	▼	Jug. Jud.	▲	
„	B.V.	▼	„	▼	
„	S.V.	▲	„	▼	
„	A.S.	▼	„	▼	
Tschechen	polit.	▼	Tsch.Jud.	▲	
„	B.V.	▼	„	▼	
„	S.V.	▲	„	▲	
„	A.S.	▼		▼	
Franzosen	polit.	▼	Fr. Jud.	▲	
„	B.V.	▼	„	▲	
„	S.V.	▲	„	▲	
„	A.S.	▼		▼	
Italiener	polit.	▼	It. Jud.	▲	
„	B.V.	▼	„	▼	
„	S.V.	▲	„	▼	
„	A.S.	▼		▼	
Andere Nat.		▼	An.Jud.	▲	
		▼		▼	
		▲			
		▼		▼	

ZUSAMMEN

One of the exhibits at the permanent exposition "Litoměřice Concentration Camp 1944–1945", placed in the former Women's Courtyard of the Small Fortress

A group statue by Jiří Sozanský on the grounds of the former crematorium
of the Litoměřice concentration camp

Mourning Hall in front of the Fourth Courtyard of the Small Fortress. It holds the earth from the main concentration camps in which prisoners from the Czech lands suffered and died during the Nazi occupation

The signboard of the Gestapo police prison is exhibited at the permanent exhibition "Terezín Small Fortress 1940–1945" in the Small Fortress Museum

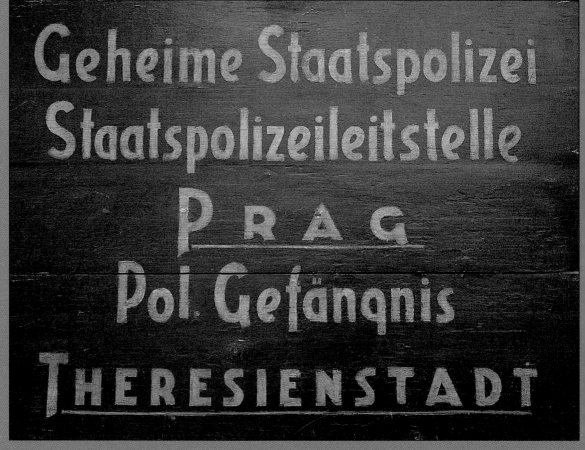

Geheime Staatspolizei
Staatspolizeileitstelle
PRAG
Pol. Gefängnis
THERESIENSTADT

A picture taken at the permanent exhibition "Terezín in the 'Final Solution of the Jewish Question' 1941–1945" in the Terezín Ghetto Museum

The Memorial Stone, donated by President of Israel Chaim Herzog in 1991. It is located in the Jewish Cemetery crematorium

Places of Suffering and Braveness

The facilities of Nazi repression in Terezín and Litoměřice

Written by

doc. PhDr. Vojtěch Blodig, CSc., Mgr. Ludmila Chládková and Miroslava Langhamerová
The documentation material used comes from the collections **of the Terezín Memorial,
the Jewish Museum in Prague** (24/1, 24/2, 24/3, 27/1, 28/1, 28/2, 35/2, 42/2, 43/1),
the National Film Archives in Prague (27/2, 39/2), **the Archives of the Ministry of Interior
of the Czech Republic** (55/1,55/2) **and Tomáš Fritta-Haas's private collection**
(12/2, 25/1, 26/2, 29/1, 30/1, 30/2, 32/2, 33/1, 33/2, 34/2).
Colour photographs by Miloslav Hušek
Black and white photographs and reprints by Jana Nováková
Graphic design by Václav Rytina
Translated into English by Petr Kurfürst
Editors in charge: Marie Vitochová and Jindřich Kejř

Published for the Terezín Memorial by Jitka Kejřová, V RÁJI Publishing
(Tomášská 10, Praha 1, Czech Republic) in 2003 as its 135th publication;
26 colour and 119 black and white photographs

First edition, Praha 2003, 2013
Printed by Východočeská tiskárna, spol. s r. o., Sezemice 2013